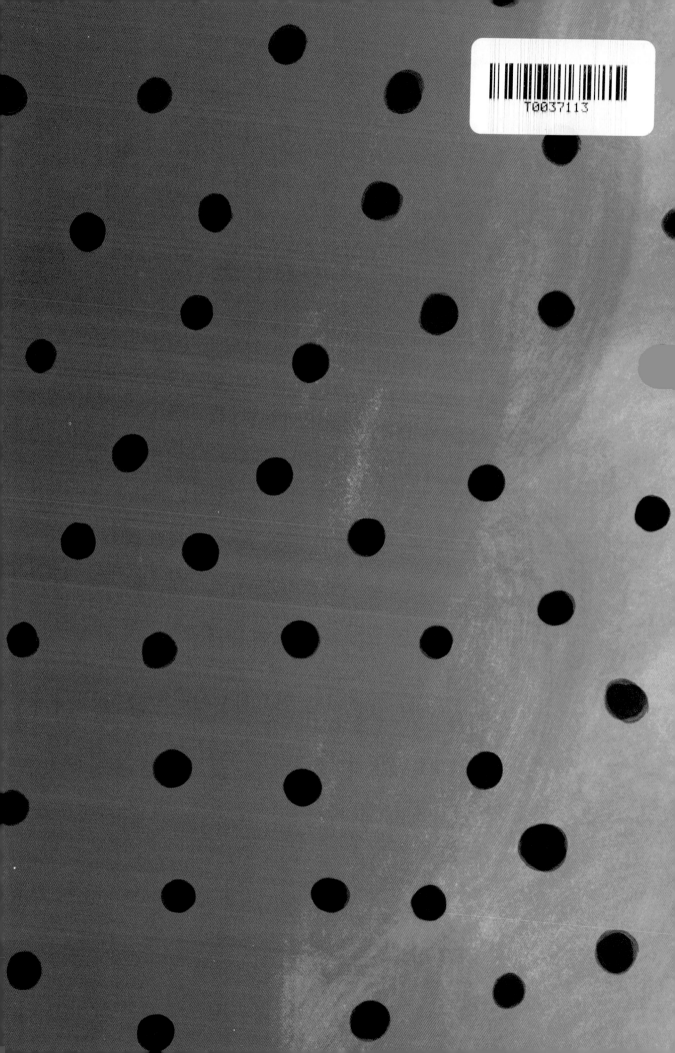

Ladybug
LAUNCH

Inspired by a True Story of Chinitas in Space

MELISSA TREMPE & NATALIA OJEDA

Illustrated by **MANUELA MONTOYA**

Margaret K. McElderry Books

New York   London   Toronto   Sydney   New Delhi

A tiny chinita and a little chica

lived in the southernmost corner of the world.

Other chinitas loved polka dots, but Luna preferred stars.

Other chicas stirred up porotos con riendas,
but Natalia stirred up experiments.

Ka-BOOM!

Luna dreamed of becoming an astronauta
in a shiny shuttle with rocket boosters.

Natalia dreamed of becoming a scientist
in a shiny lab with bubbling beakers.

Yet as Luna grew older, she never saw a chinita astronauta.

"I could be the first!" she told the others.

"Unlikely," said an amigo. "Stop dreaming and eat your dinner."

Luna eyed the swarm of tiny aphids. The pests could destroy a garden. Eating them was importante *and* delicioso— but in her heart, Luna wanted *más*.

Natalia grew older, never knowing anyone who attended a university.

Could I be the first in my familia? she wondered. While Papá and Mamá worked, she watched her little brothers. They were happy, but in her heart, Natalia wanted *más*.

As chinitas chased aphids, Luna chased her dream.
"Three (tres) . . . two (dos) . . . one (uno) . . . BLASTOFF!"

As amigos played outside, Natalia watched
her brothers and studied.

But space travel had its challenges. . . .

"EEK! Returning to Earth!"

Luna crashed down . . .

as Natalia climbed up. . . .

"Gotcha!
Now, I'd better
get to school!"

When Luna wiggled her way out, the city park was gone.
A swarm of humans sat at desks listening to their teacher.

"If YOU'RE our future scientists . . ." (Natalia sat straighter.)
"And SPACE is the future . . ." (Luna's antennae tingled.)
"Then let's create an experiment for space!" said Miss Martínez.

This was all Natalia wanted and más. Her hand shot in the air as ideas flew around the room.

Outer space *and* aphids. It was all Luna wanted and más!
She mustered her courage and fluttered forward. . . .

"I can save plants from pests. Send me to space!"
No one understood, but everyone saw.

"Chinitas catch and eat aphids!" said Carolina.

"But could they in zero gravity?" asked Claudia.

Natalia smiled at Luna. "If they can, astronautas could grow food while chinitas keep the pests away!"

Las chicas wanted to know más, and Luna was hungry to help. They designed terrariums. Grew plants. Added aphids.

"Now," said Luna importantly, "watch how I catch aphids on Earth."

Natalia set timers. Took measurements. Counted insectos.

"Wow! She eats fifty aphids a day!"

Natalia felt like a real scientist. Luna felt stuffed!

"I'm ready!" said a plump Luna. "Take me to your spaceship."

There was no ship, but there was an idea. "What if," said Miss Martínez, "we ask NASA to take our experiment on a mission to space?"

"NASA? The largest space program in the world?" asked Natalia.

"But we're just a class of kids from Chile," said an amiga.

"Sí, the odds are against us," said their teacher.
"Should we give up? Return to our textbooks?"
"¡NO!" Las chicas and a tiny chinita wanted *más*.

So Luna and two students boarded a plane . . .
"¡Adiós!"
Flew from one hemisphere to the other . . .
"¡Hola!"
And met with NASA.

"If astronautas farm in space . . . ," said Maritza.
"Could chinitas be used as a safe and natural pest control?" finished Cristina.
"Sí, send me to space!" chirped Luna.

Back home in Chile, an answer arrived.

Natalia cheered! Luna clapped her wings! But Miss Martínez frowned. "We'll have to provide the equipment, insectos, plantas, *and* prove to scientists our experiment will work in space."

"We can do it!" said Natalia.

"Sí," said Miss Martínez. "But we'll need money. Lots of it."

Las chicas didn't have money. But they had grit. *Lots* of it.

Natalia and her amigas grabbed jars and headed to sporting events.

"Can chinitas catch aphids in zero gravity? Help us find out!"

As their jars filled with money, their hearts filled with hope.

Soon they needed más insectos.
Natalia placed tin cans in every window
at home to breed chinitas.

Luna helped look after the littles.

The time came to prove the experiment would work in space. Natalia never knew anyone who flew across the world to an American university, to stand before scientists, to simulate a space-ready experiment. . . .

But *she* could be the first.

Natalia's voice rang steady and strong, just like a real scientist.

On July 23, 1999, space shuttle *Columbia* pointed skyward. On board were astronauta Eileen Collins — the first woman to command a NASA mission — and one very important experiment designed by unstoppable chicas from Chile.

Columbia's rocket boosters rumbled, and the world counted in every language, "Three . . . two . . . one . . . LIFTOFF!"

From above, a chinita astronauta looked down.

From below, a young scientist looked up.
Already dreaming of the future . . .
determined to make it *más*.

Author Note from Natalia

Natalia is inspired by my personal experience, but her story is for all the chicas who worked on the chinita project. We grew up in Santiago, Chile, and attended a modest all-girls school. I dreamed of becoming a doctor, but I often worried my dream was too big. My father worked as a waiter. When my mother cleaned homes, I watched my little brothers. No one in my familia had attended college. How could I? It's funny how something as small as a chinita could change everything.

It started when our science teacher, Miss Ivonne Martínez, learned about a Chilean satellite that might launch student-led experiments. She challenged the class three years ahead of me to devise an experiment, and the chinita idea was born.

When Dr. Franklin Chang Díaz, an astronaut for NASA, spoke at our planetarium, Miss Martínez took a chance. She told him about our project, and he believed in the experiment. He believed in *us*. In 1997, students Maritza Hernandez and Cristina Oyarzun presented the idea to NASA. The scientists saw value in finding a natural pest control for farming in space, and our chinita project was a go!

Natalia with astronaut Dr. Franklin Chang Díaz.

Natalia Ojeda (15) at the University of Colorado, where she and Natalia Castillo simulated the experiment for scientists.

Natalia at the hospital, ready to help patients.

Natalia with her four daughters.

NASA helped with costs, but we needed money. The Chilean Air Force and others joined our efforts and helped us raise over one hundred thousand dollars. For over three years, we studied chinita behavior and development. At home, I bred chinitas in tin cans in nearly every window of the house. In the winter, I brought them into my bedroom to keep them warm. As I watched the beetles grow, my confidence grew with them. If a group of chicas from Chile could make an impact on science for NASA, what else was possible?

The time came to simulate the experiment for scientists, and Natalia Castillo and I were chosen! (Sí, dos Natalias!) I was only fifteen when we flew to the University of Colorado, and I was full of nerves, but we succeeded! Perhaps I could do *anything*.

On July 23, 1999, four chinitas rocketed into space. My dear amiga Claudia Flores named them John, Paul, Ringo, and George after the famous band members of the Beatles. Two classmates attended the launch, and I listened over the radio with countless proud Chilean citizens. That day, astronaut Eileen Collins made history as NASA's first female mission commander. Sí, anything seemed possible.

But could our chinitas control the swarm of aphids in zero gravity? Could I really become a doctor? Like many chicas throughout history, we were resilient. We were determined. And we succeeded. One day in the future, if people farm in space, chinita astronautas will likely be on board. And one day in the future, YOU could do *anything* too.

—NATALIA OJEDA, doctor of the Palliative Care Unit
of San Juan de Dios Hospital, Santiago, Chile

Spanish to English Glossary

abuela—grandmother

adiós—good-bye

ay—oh

amigo/amiga—friend (masculine/feminine)

astronauta—astronaut (feminine)

chica—girl

chinita—used in Chile to mean *ladybug*.
Other Spanish-speaking countries use the word *mariquita*.

delicioso—delicious

excelente—excellent

familia—family

hola—hello

importante—important

insectos—insects

mamá—mom

más—more

papá—dad

plantas—plants

porotos con riendas—a traditional soup made in Chile

sí—yes

uno, dos, tres—one, two, three

Calling all curious kids! Continue your exploration:

Ladybugs aren't actually bugs! Find more fascinating facts about these insects by going to rangerrick.org or kids.nationalgeographic.com. Type LADYBUG in the search bar to find articles and activities.

Colonel Eileen Collins served as NASA's first female mission commander on July 23, 1999. Learn about her and other great women in science and space at chandra.harvard.edu/women/story.html.

Chandra X-ray Observatory was launched into space by Colonel Eileen Collins and her crew. They hoped it would send images to Earth for five years. Yet over twenty years later, Chandra has been capturing images of exploded stars, black holes, and other galaxies. See these incredible images at chandra.harvard.edu/photo/.

For Mom—no matter how small I was, you believed I could do big things.

And for Emma and William—shoot for the stars; I know you'll make it.

—M. T.

For my parents, who gave me an example of work, honesty, and faith.

And for my daughters, who I love with all my heart.

—N. O.

To the curious girls in Latin America.

—M. M.

MARGARET K. McELDERRY BOOKS
An imprint of Simon & Schuster Children's Publishing Division
1230 Avenue of the Americas, New York, New York 10020
Text © 2024 by Dr. Natalia Ojeda and Melissa Trempe
Illustration © 2024 by Manuela Montoya
Book design by Greg Stadnyk © 2024 by Simon & Schuster, Inc.
All rights reserved, including the right of reproduction in whole or in part in any form.
MARGARET K. McELDERRY BOOKS is a trademark of Simon & Schuster, Inc.
Simon & Schuster: Celebrating 100 Years of Publishing in 2024
For information about special discounts for bulk purchases, please contact Simon & Schuster Special Sales at
1-866-506-1949 or business@simonandschuster.com.
The Simon & Schuster Speakers Bureau can bring authors to your live event. For more information or to book an event,
contact the Simon & Schuster Speakers Bureau at 1-866-248-3049 or visit our website at www.simonspeakers.com.
The text for this book was set in Excelsior.
The illustrations for this book were rendered digitally.
Manufactured in China
1223 SCP
First Edition
2 4 6 8 10 9 7 5 3 1
Library of Congress Cataloging-in-Publication Data
Names: Trempe, Melissa, author. | Ojeda, Natalia, author. | Montoya, Manu, illustrator.
Title: Ladybug launch : inspired by a true story of chinitas in space / Melissa Trempe & Natalia Ojeda ;
illustrated by Manuela Montoya.
Description: First edition. | New York : Margaret K. McElderry Books, [2024] | Audience: Ages 4–8. | Audience: Grades 2–3. |
Summary: Luna, a ladybug who dreams of becoming an astronaut, teams up with Natalia,
a girl who aspires to be a scientist. Includes author note and Spanish to English glossary.
Identifiers: LCCN 2023010763 (print) | LCCN 2023010764 (ebook) | ISBN 9781665930406 (hardcover) |
ISBN 9781665930413 (ebook)
Subjects: CYAC: Ladybugs—Fiction. | Science—Experiments—Fiction. | Ambition—Fiction. | LCGFT: Picture books.
Classification: LCC PZ7.1.T7454 Lad 2024 (print) | LCC PZ7.1.T7454 (ebook) | DDC [E]—dc23
LC record available at https://lccn.loc.gov/2023010763
LC ebook record available at https://lccn.loc.gov/2023010764